RECORDED VERSIONS
GUITAR

AUTHENTIC TRANSCRIPTIONS
WITH NOTES AND TABLATURE

SUM★41
All Killer No Filler

Music transcriptions by Pete Billmann and Jeff Jacobson

ISBN 0-634-03650-5

HAL•LEONARD®
CORPORATION
7777 W. BLUEMOUND RD. P.O. BOX 13819 MILWAUKEE, WI 53213

Visit Hal Leonard Online at
www.halleonard.com

CONTENTS

Nothing on My Back

Words and Music by Sum 41

* Chord symbols reflect overall harmony.

Never Wake Up

Words and Music by Sum 41

Fat Lip

Words and Music by Sum 41

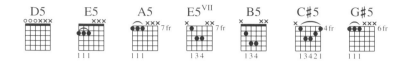

Drop D tuning:
(low to high) D–A–D–G–B–E

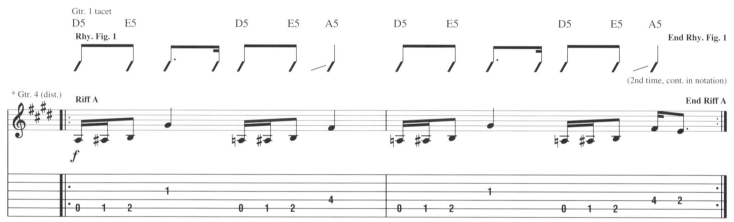

* Composite arrangement

* Doubled throughout

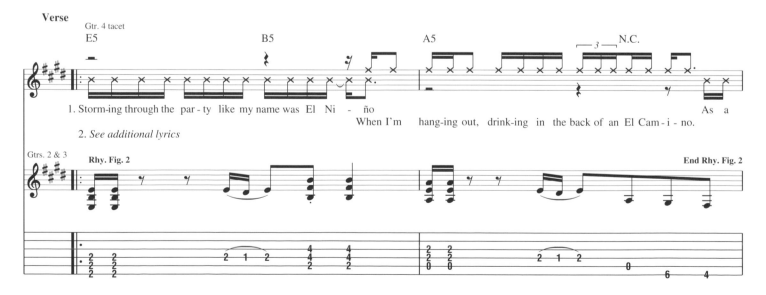

1. Storm-ing through the par-ty like my name was El Ni - ño

When I'm hang-ing out, drink-ing in the back of an El Cam-i-no. As a

2. *See additional lyrics*

Pre-Chorus
Double-time feel

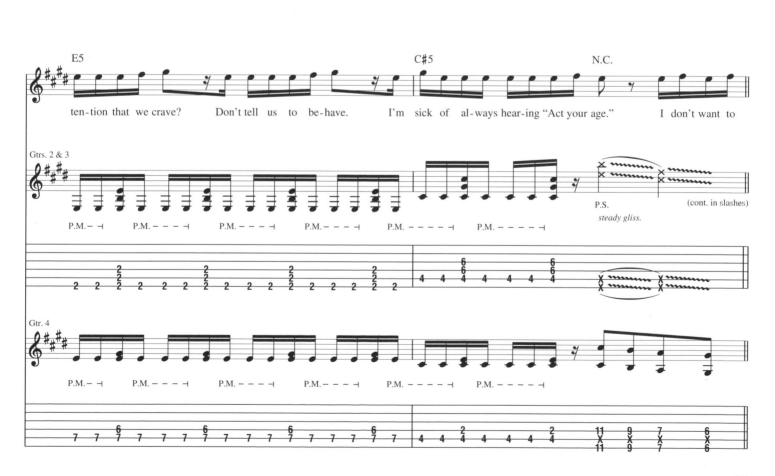

* w/ delay repeats.

Additional Lyrics

2. Because you don't
   Know us at all, we laugh when old people fall.
   But what would you expect with a conscience so small?
   Heavy Metal and mullets, it's how we were raised.
   Maiden and Priest were the gods that we praised.

2nd Pre-Chorus:
'Cause we like having fun at other people's expense and
Cutting people down is just a minor offense then.
It's none of your concern, I guess I'll never learn.
I'm sick of being told to wait my turn.
I don't want to...

Rhythms

Words and Music by Sum 41

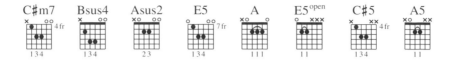

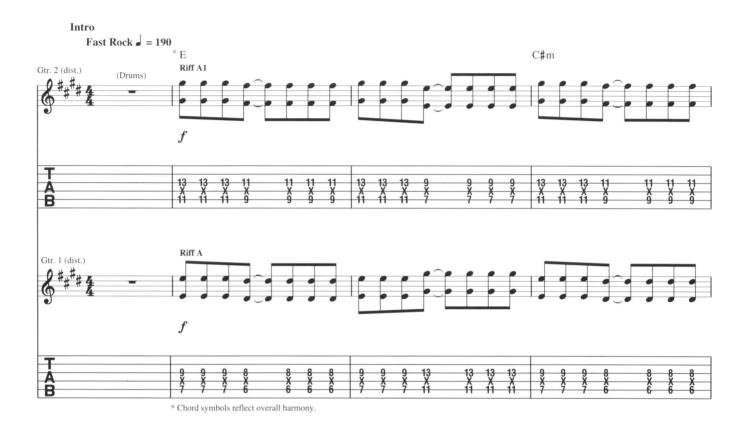

* Chord symbols reflect overall harmony.

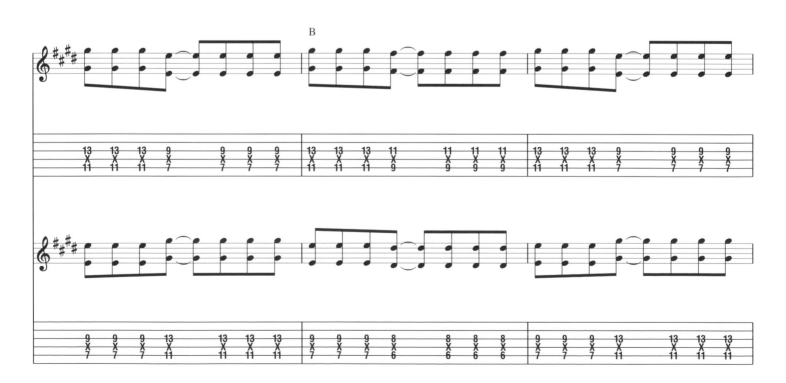

bet - ter off an - y - way. Some - how it's nev - er up to me.

End Rhy. Fig. 1

— What if I ___ would _ say? Sim - ple words, I can't re - late. _

__ I don't place up - on your view. _ It's the rhy - thms that you go through.

Chorus

I know what I want. ___ You just take me through the mo - tions.

Rhy. Fig. 2

End Rhy. Fig. 2

I know what I want, and that's more than you can say.

Post-Chorus

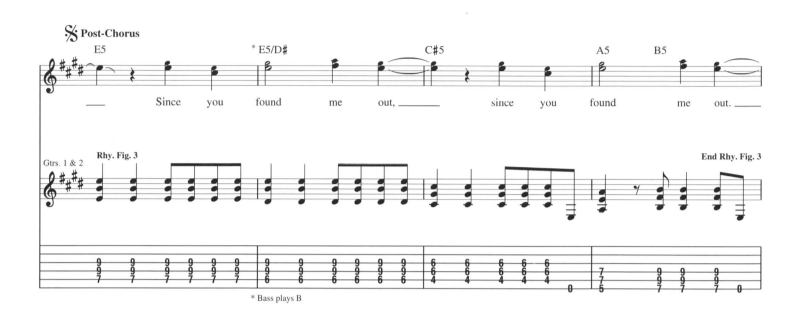

Since you found me out, since you found me out.

* Bass plays B

Since you found me out, since you found me out.

** Bass plays G#.

Interlude

1st time, Gtrs. 1 & 2: w/ Riffs A & A1
2nd time, Gtrs. 1 & 2: w/ Riffs A & A1 (1st 7 meas.)

To Coda

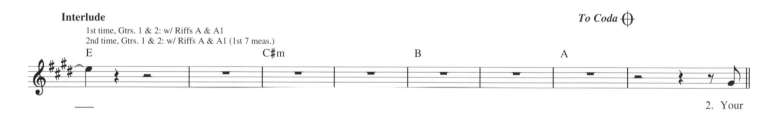

2. Your

Verse

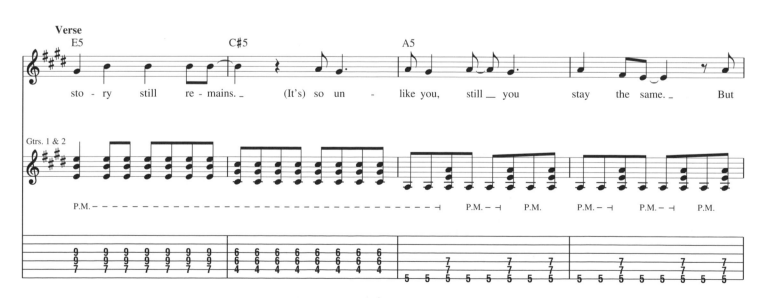

story still re-mains. (It's) so un-like you, still you stay the same. But

would - n't   do, ____   it makes   no   sense,   it's that   rhy - thms   that   you   go   through.

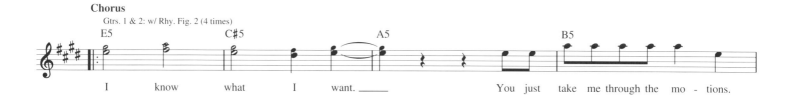

Chorus

Gtrs. 1 & 2: w/ Rhy. Fig. 2 (4 times)

I   know   what   I   want. ____   You   just   take   me through the   mo - tions.

I   know   what   I   want, ____   and that's   more   than you __ can say.   more   than you __ can say. ____

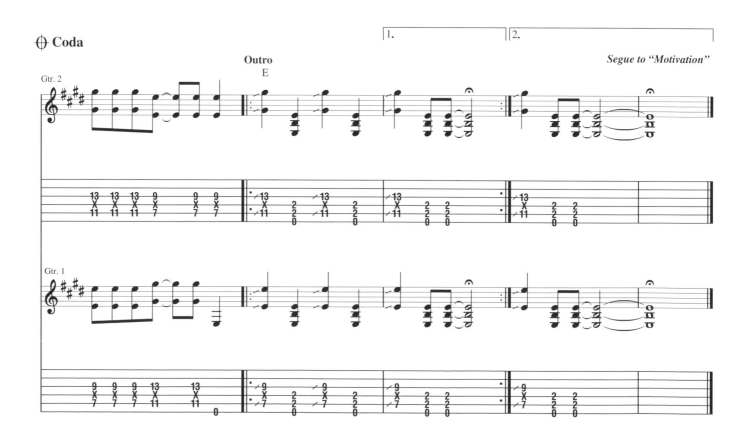

Motivation

Words and Music by Sum 41

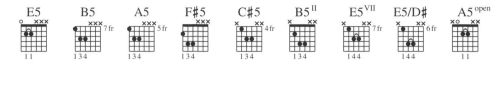

Interlude

said?

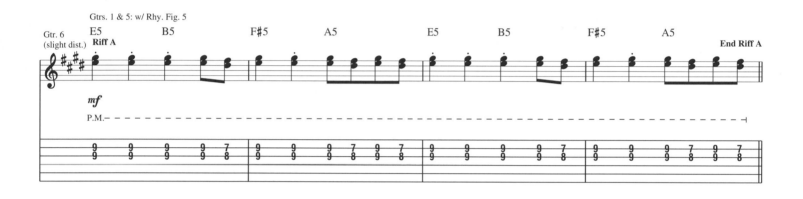

Chorus

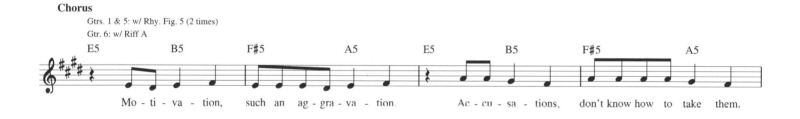

Mo - ti - va - tion, such an ag - gra - va - tion. Ac - cu - sa - tions, don't know how to take them.

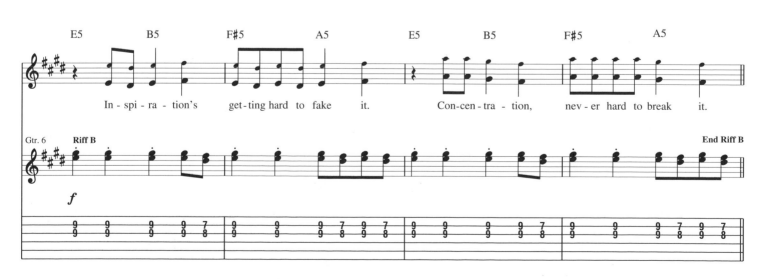

In - spi - ra - tion's get - ting hard to fake it. Con-cen - tra - tion, nev - er hard to break it.

In Too Deep

Words and Music by Sum 41

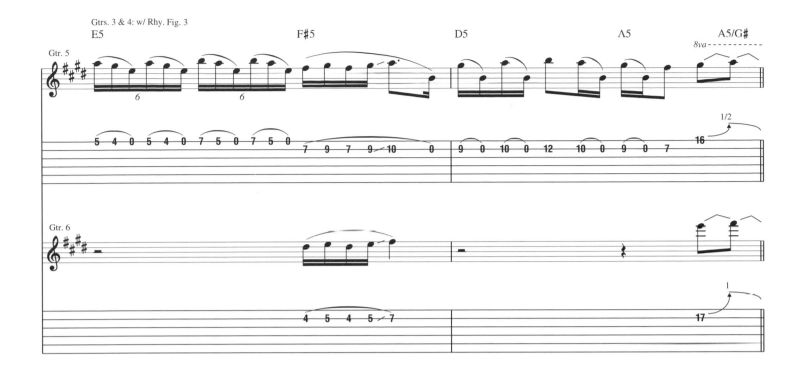

Bridge

I can't sit back and __ won - der why. __ It took so long for __ this to die. __

45

Summer

Words and Music by Sum 41

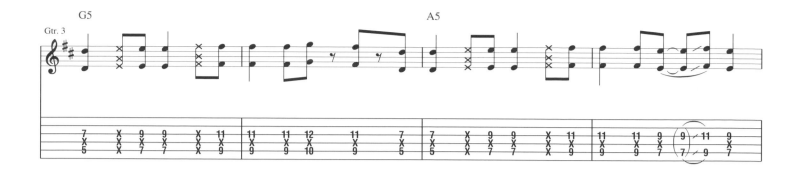

Verse

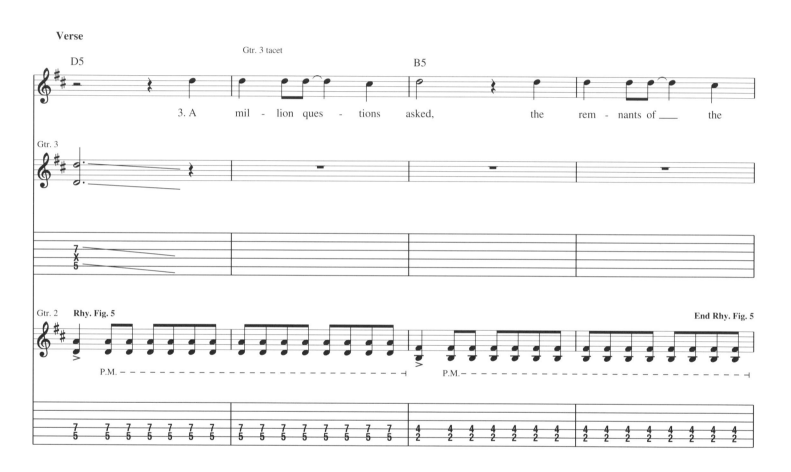

3. A mil-lion ques-tions asked, the rem-nants of ___ the past. You've al-ways been ___ de-nied, but al-ways by ___ your

Handle This

Words and Music by Sum 41

Drop D tuning:
(low to high) D–A–D–G–B–E

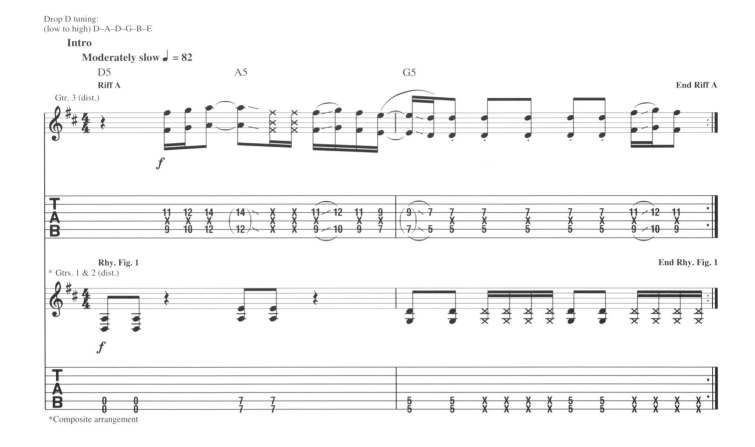

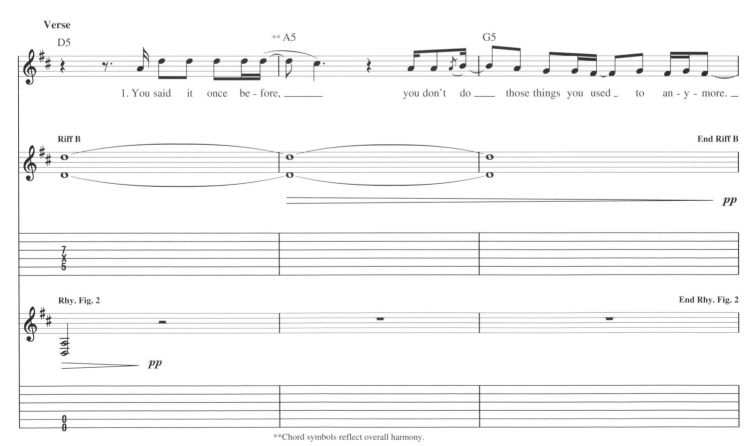

*Chord symbols reflect overall harmony.

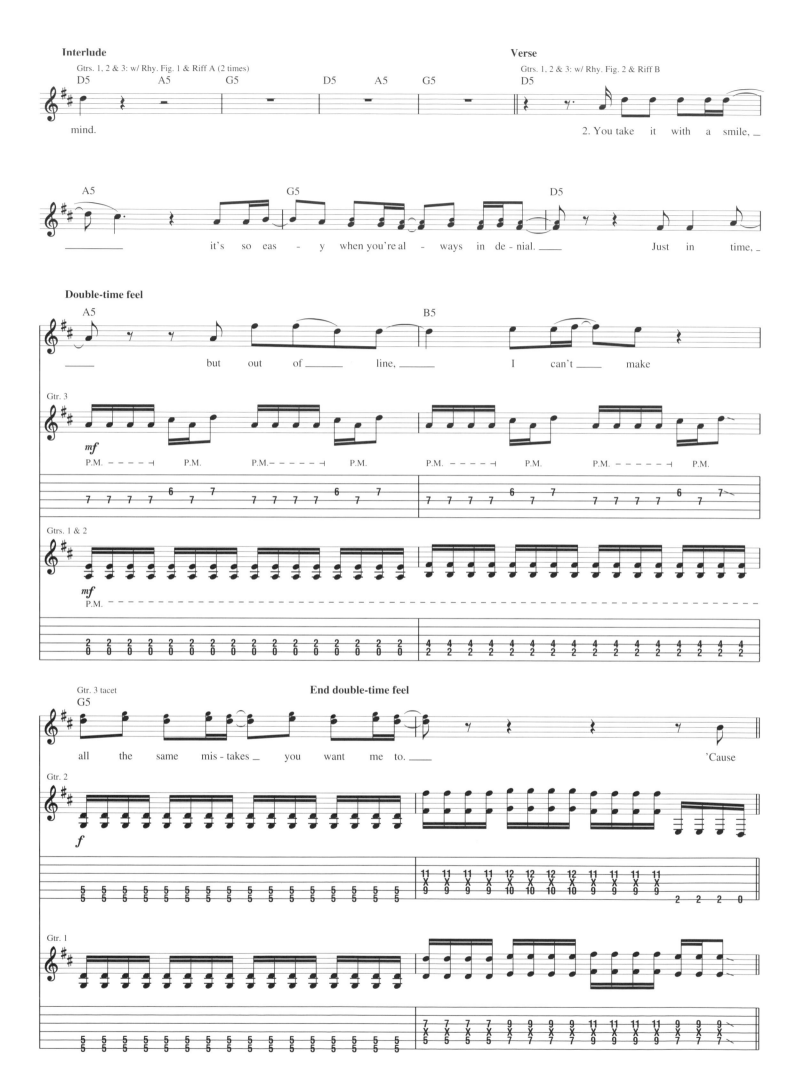

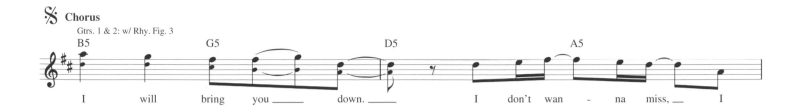

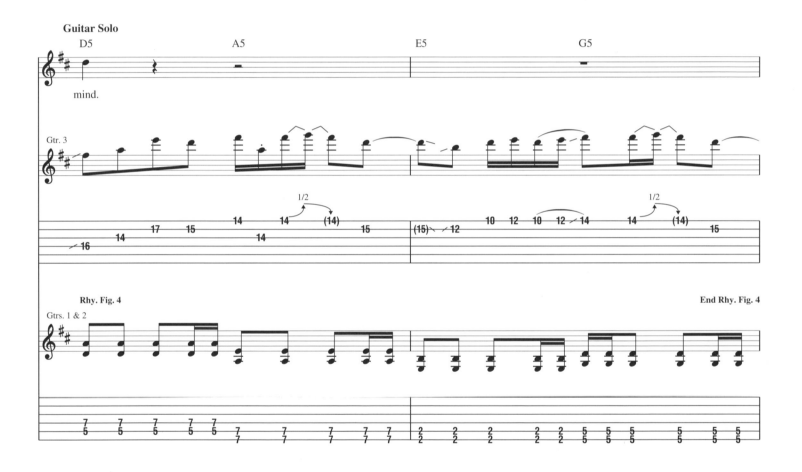

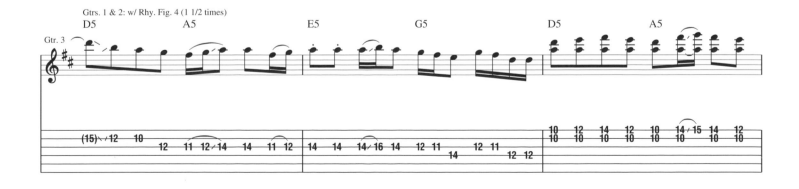

Bridge

You're giv-ing up, you know it's not what you need. _

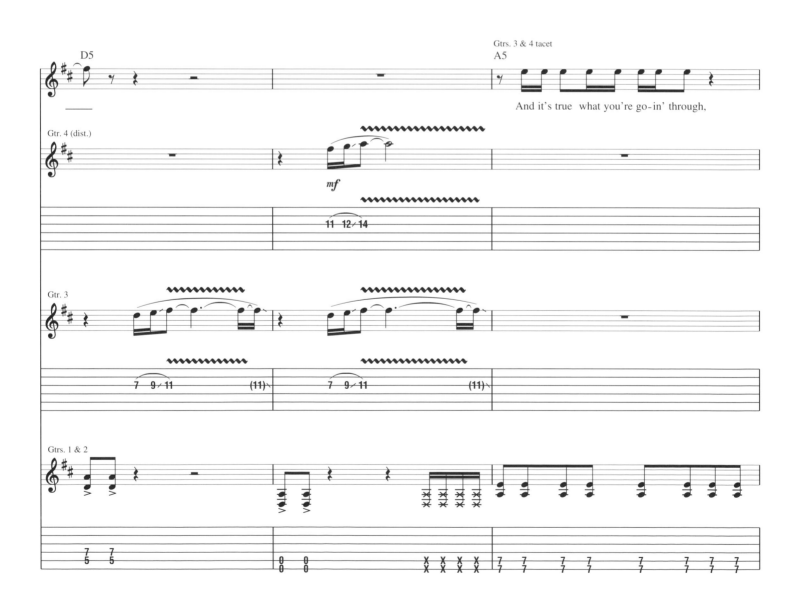

And it's true what you're go-in' through,

59

Nev-er thought it'd ev-er come to this, in fact, was nev-er what you

want-ed from me, or how you meant it to be.

Crazy Amanda Bunkface

Words and Music by Sum 41

Chorus

hear   you bitch   no   more.   I   was bet-ter   off   a   year   be-fore.   No   mat-ter how   I

* Gtrs. 1 & 2 (dist.)

Rhy. Fig. 2

f

* Composite arrangement

try,   I   can't   ig-nore.   Ev-'ry time I   think,   my brain   gets   sore   when I'm with

End Rhy. Fig. 2

Interlude

you.

Rhy. Fig. 3

End Rhy. Fig. 3

Gtrs. 1 & 2: w/ Rhy. Fig. 3

G5   D/F♯ G5   C5   D5

* Chord symbols reflect implied harmony.

All She's Got

Words and Music by Sum 41

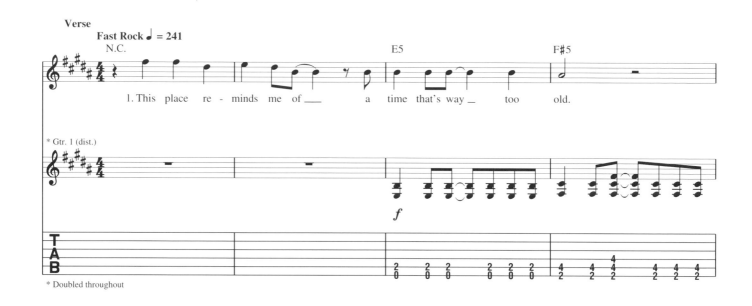

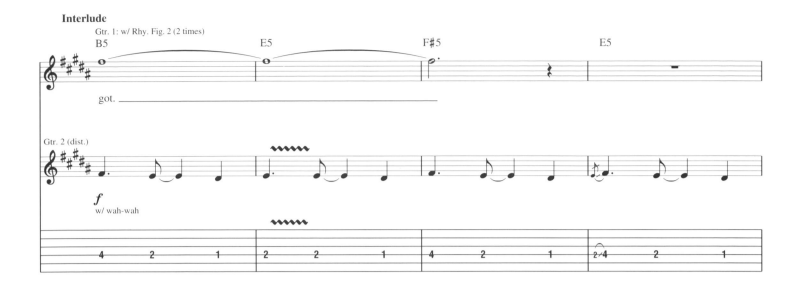

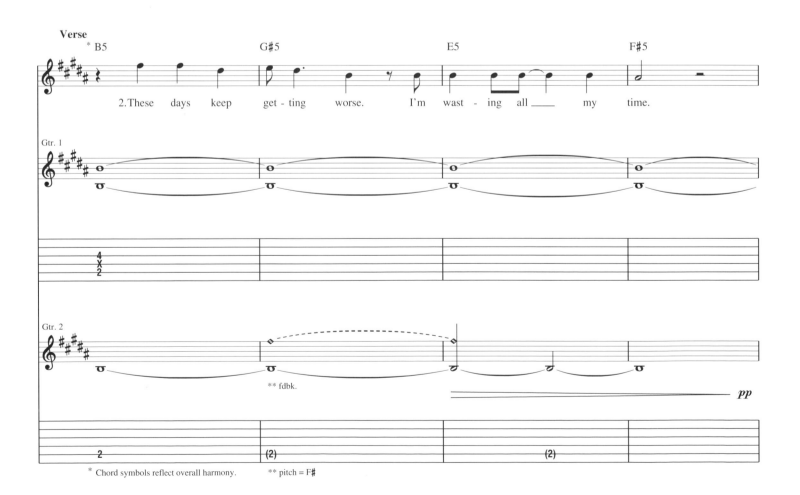

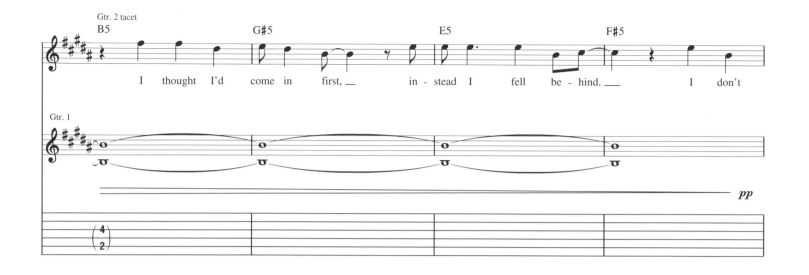

I thought I'd come in first, __ in - stead I fell be - hind. ___ I don't

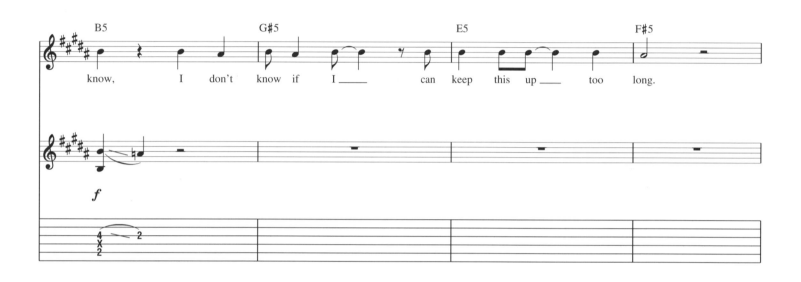

know, I don't know if I ____ can keep this up ___ too long.

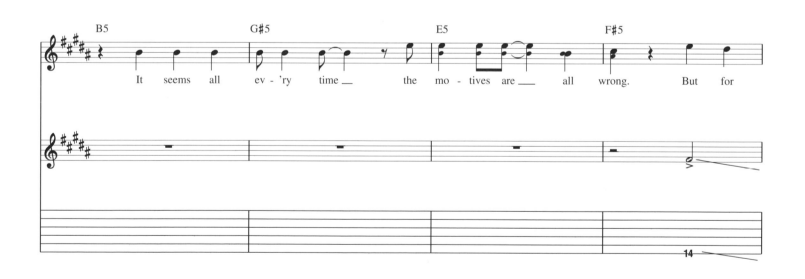

It seems all ev - 'ry time __ the mo - tives are ___ all wrong. But for

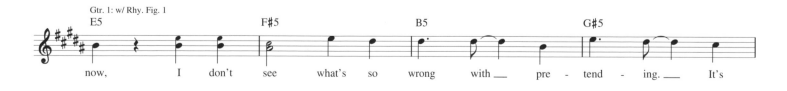

now, I don't see what's so wrong with __ pre - tend - ing. ___ It's

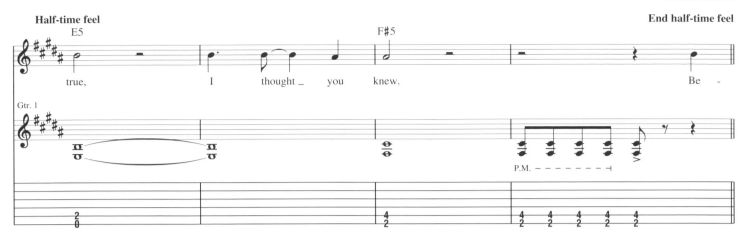

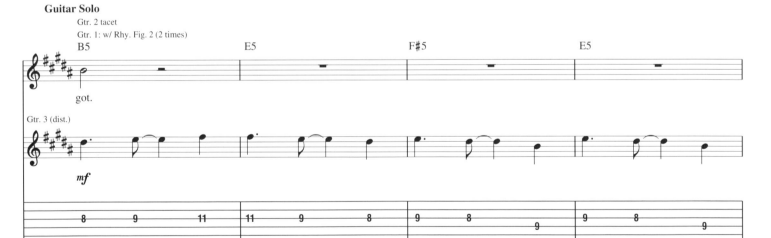

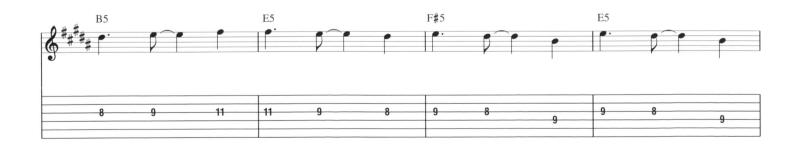

Bridge
Half-time feel

It's times like this, _____
(But time's run _____ out,
it's

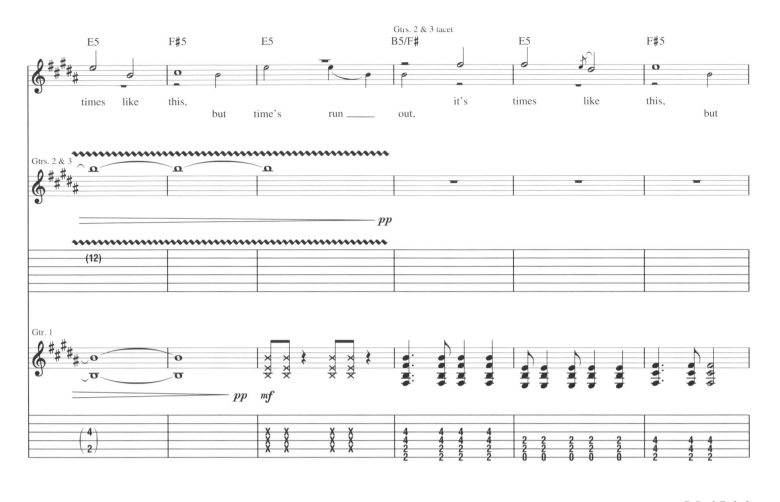

times like this, but time's run _____ out, it's times like this, but

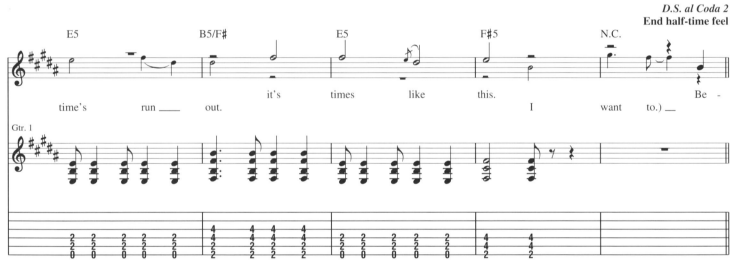

time's run _____ out. it's times like this. I want to.) _____ Be -

D.S. al Coda 2
End half-time feel

⊕ Coda 2

Segue to "Heart Attack"

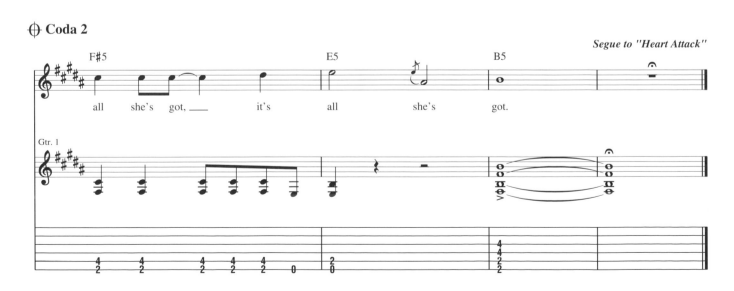

all she's got, _____ it's all she's got.

Heart Attack

Words and Music by Sum 41

Interlude

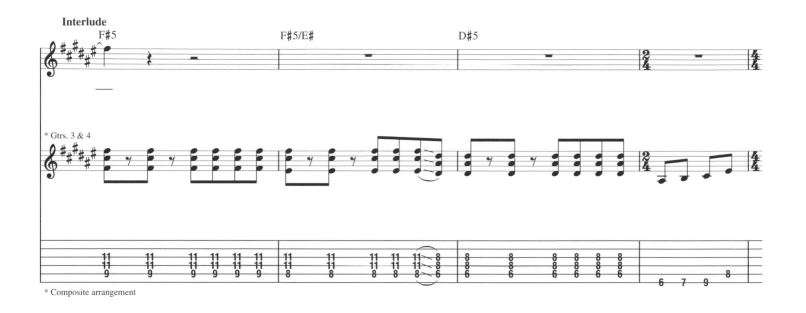

* Gtrs. 3 & 4

* Composite arrangement

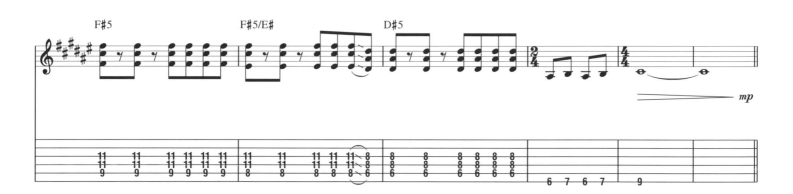

Verse

Gtr. 1: w/ Riff A (2 times)
Gtrs. 3 & 4 tacet

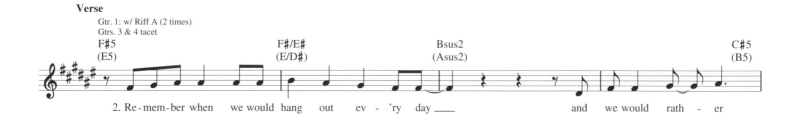

2. Re-mem-ber when we would hang out ev-'ry day ___ and we would rath - er

Gtrs. 3 & 4

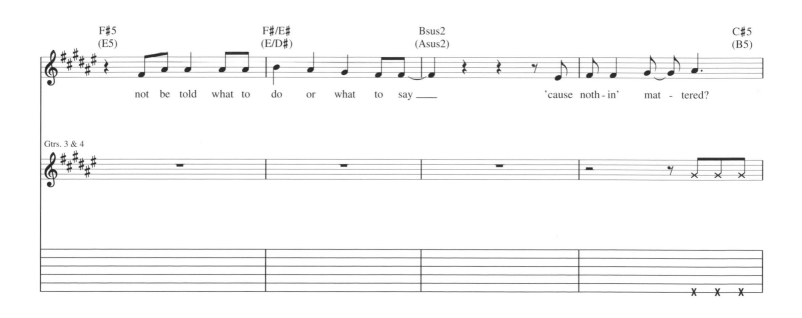

not be told what to do or what to say ___ 'cause noth-in' mat - tered?

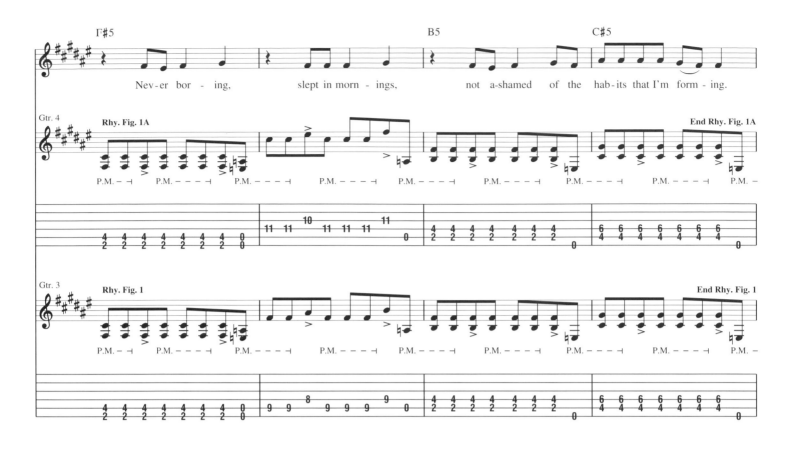

Nev-er bor - ing,   slept in morn - ings,   not a-shamed   of the hab-its that I'm form - ing.

It's not im-por-tant   if days are short-ened. I   can't make   time when   noth-in's   new 'cause

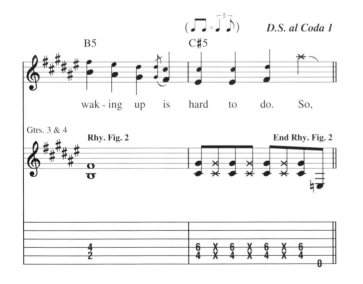

wak-ing   up   is   hard   to   do.   So,

D.S. al Coda 1

⊕ **Coda 1**

Pain for Pleasure

Words and Music by Sum 41

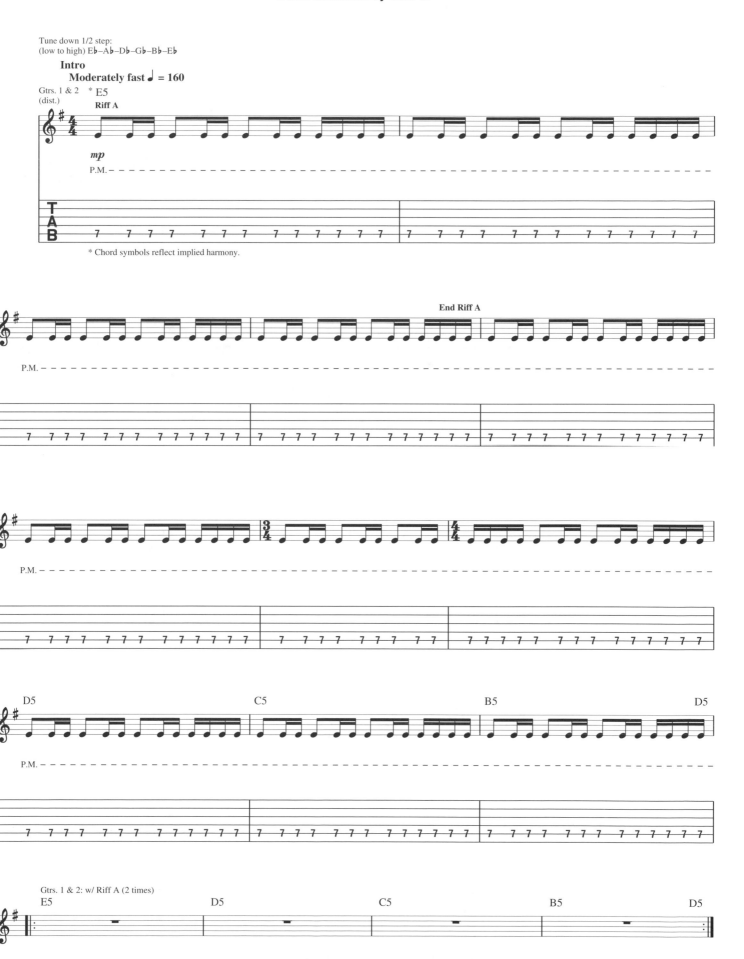

* Composite arrangement.

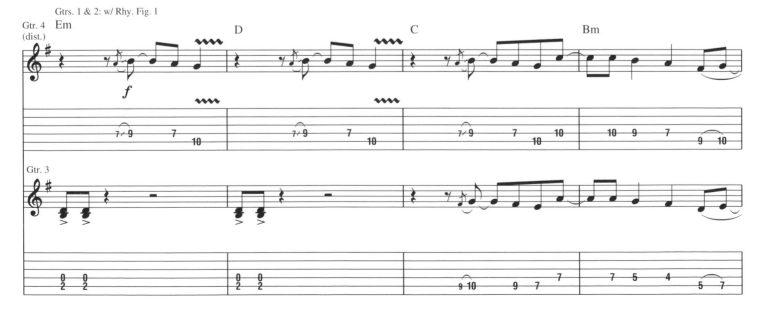

Verse

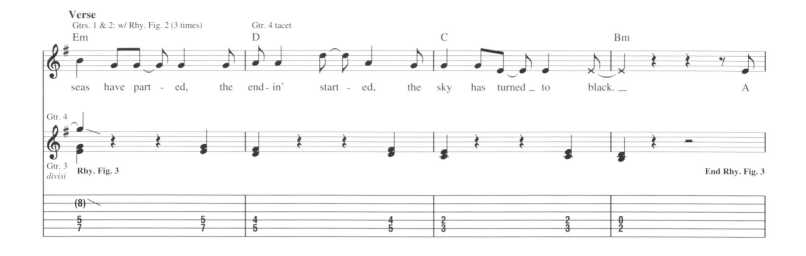

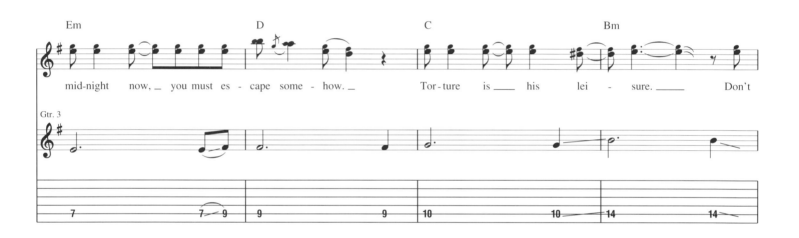

Guitar Notation Legend

Guitar Music can be notated three different ways: on a *musical staff*, in *tablature*, and in *rhythm slashes*.

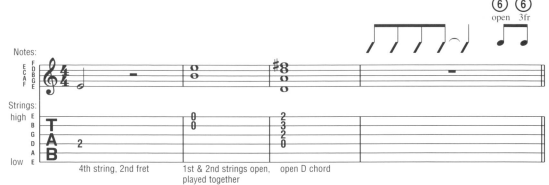

RHYTHM SLASHES are written above the staff. Strum chords in the rhythm indicated. Use the chord diagrams found at the top of the first page of the transcription for the appropriate chord voicings. Round noteheads indicate single notes.

THE MUSICAL STAFF shows pitches and rhythms and is divided by bar lines into measures. Pitches are named after the first seven letters of the alphabet.

TABLATURE graphically represents the guitar fingerboard. Each horizontal line represents a string, and each number represents a fret.

4th string, 2nd fret

1st & 2nd strings open, played together

open D chord

HALF-STEP BEND: Strike the note and bend up 1/2 step.

WHOLE-STEP BEND: Strike the note and bend up one step.

GRACE NOTE BEND: Strike the note and immediately bend up as indicated.

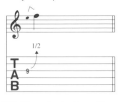

SLIGHT (MICROTONE) BEND: Strike the note and bend up 1/4 step.

BEND AND RELEASE: Strike the note and bend up as indicated, then release back to the original note. Only the first note is struck.

PRE-BEND: Bend the note as indicated, then strike it.

VIBRATO: The string is vibrated by rapidly bending and releasing the note with the fretting hand.

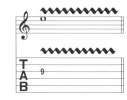

WIDE VIBRATO: The pitch is varied to a greater degree by vibrating with the fretting hand.

HAMMER-ON: Strike the first (lower) note with one finger, then sound the higher note (on the same string) with another finger by fretting it without picking.

PULL-OFF: Place both fingers on the notes to be sounded. Strike the first note and without picking, pull the finger off to sound the second (lower) note.

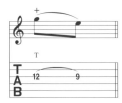

LEGATO SLIDE: Strike the first note and then slide the same fret-hand finger up or down to the second note. The second note is not struck.

SHIFT SLIDE: Same as legato slide, except the second note is struck.

TRILL: Very rapidly alternate between the notes indicated by continuously hammering on and pulling off.

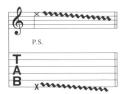

TAPPING: Hammer ("tap") the fret indicated with the pick-hand index or middle finger and pull off to the note fretted by the fret hand.

NATURAL HARMONIC: Strike the note while the fret-hand lightly touches the string directly over the fret indicated.

PINCH HARMONIC: The note is fretted normally and a harmonic is produced by adding the edge of the thumb or the tip of the index finger of the pick hand to the normal pick attack.

PICK SCRAPE: The edge of the pick is rubbed down (or up) the string, producing a scratchy sound.

MUFFLED STRINGS: A percussive sound is produced by laying the fret hand across the string(s) without depressing, and striking them with the pick hand.

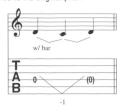

PALM MUTING: The note is partially muted by the pick hand lightly touching the string(s) just before the bridge.

RAKE: Drag the pick across the strings indicated with a single motion.

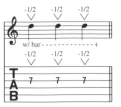

TREMOLO PICKING: The note is picked as rapidly and continuously as possible.

VIBRATO BAR DIVE AND RETURN: The pitch of the note or chord is dropped a specified number of steps (in rhythm) then returned to the original pitch.

VIBRATO BAR SCOOP: Depress the bar just before striking the note, then quickly release the bar.

VIBRATO BAR DIP: Strike the note and then immediately drop a specified number of steps, then release back to the original pitch.